Flav...
W...

RECIPES

C000151729

Compiled by Julia Skinner

THE FRANCIS FRITH COLLECTION

www.francisfrith.com

First published in the United Kingdom in 2011 by The Francis Frith Collection®

This edition published exclusively for Identity Books in 2011 ISBN 978-1-84589-553-2

British Library Cataloguing in Publication Data

Flavours of Wales - Recipes
Compiled by Julia Skinner

The Francis Frith Collection
Unit 6, Oakley Business Park,
Wylye Road, Dinton,
Wiltshire SP3 5EU
Tel: +44 (0) 1722 716 376
Email: info@francisfrith.co.uk
www.francisfrith.com

Printed and bound in Malaysia

Front Cover: **CARMARTHEN, CORACLES 1898** 41093p
Frontispiece: **CENARTH, CORACLE FISHING c1960** C376016

The colour-tinting is for illustrative purposes only, and is not intended to be historically accurate

CONTENTS

RECIPE

LEEK BROTH – CAWL CENNIN

'Cawl' is a Welsh word (pronounced like 'foul', rather than 'shawl') for which there is no definitive translation. It signifies 'broth' or 'soup', but a cawl is so much more than just a simple soup – it is a filling meal that would originally have been cooked in an iron pot over an open fire, made up of whatever ingredients were available at the time, such as pieces of bacon, scraps of mutton or lamb, cabbage, swede, carrots, potatoes, leeks and any other seasonal vegetables. Cawl can be eaten all together, with the meat and broth served in a bowl at the same time, but in many Welsh homes the broth is served first and the meat and vegetables are eaten afterwards. The soup in this recipe is best made using the stock in which a piece of bacon or ham has been boiled. The addition of oatmeal is the traditional Welsh way of thickening broth.

900ml/1½ pints of stock – ham or bacon stock if possible
225g/8oz potatoes, peeled and diced
225g/8oz carrots, diced
2 leeks, washed, trimmed and sliced
Half a small cabbage, shredded
2 tablespoonfuls oatmeal
Salt and freshly ground black pepper
Chopped fresh parsley

Put the stock in a large saucepan, and add the diced potatoes and carrots. Bring to the boil, then reduce the heat and cook for 10 minutes. Add the sliced leeks and shredded cabbage. Mix the oatmeal with a little water and add to the broth. Bring it to the boil again, then reduce the heat and simmer for 10-15 minutes, until the vegetables are cooked. Season to taste with salt and freshly ground black pepper. Serve in individual soup bowls, sprinkled with chopped fresh parsley.

PANTASAPH, THE ROAD TO THE VILLAGE
c1940 P193057

RECIPE

TREGARON GRANNY'S BROTH –
CAWL MAMGU TREGARON

675g/1½ lbs bacon, cut into small pieces
450g/1 lb shin of beef, trimmed of fat and cut into
    small pieces
450g/1 lb potatoes, peeled and diced
225g/8oz parsnips, peeled and diced
225g/8oz carrots, peeled and diced
1 white cabbage, stalk removed, shredded
1 large leek, washed, trimmed and chopped into
    small pieces
2 tablespoonfuls oatmeal
Salt and freshly ground black pepper

Place the bacon, beef and all the vegetables except the leek in a large saucepan and cover with cold water. Add salt and freshly ground black pepper to taste. Bring to the boil, then carefully skim the surface. Reduce the heat, cover the pan and leave to simmer gently for 2½ hours.

Mix the oatmeal with a little water and stir it into the broth, to thicken it a little. Add the chopped leek. Bring the broth to the boil again, then reduce the heat and simmer for a further 15-20 minutes, until the leek is cooked. Adjust the seasoning if necessary, and serve the broth piping hot, with crusty bread.

BANGOR, HIGH STREET 1908 60733

RECIPE

GRILLED GRAYLING

Wales has a wealth of rivers, lakes and reservoirs set in stunning scenery, where a wide variety of fish can be caught. Salmon, sea trout and wild brown trout are abundant, and the rivers of south Wales have a reputation for the quality of their grayling. Grayling is a small freshwater fish similar to a brown trout. It has an excellent flavour but does not keep very well after it is caught, so should be eaten as soon as possible.

> 4 good-sized grayling
> 1 tablespoonful of fresh herbs such as chervil,
>   chives, tarragon and parsley
> 115g/4oz butter, softened to room temperature
> Salt and pepper

Clean the fish thoroughly, and make two diagonal slits to the bone on both sides with a sharp knife. Chop the herbs finely and mix them with the softened butter, and season the mixture with salt and pepper. Smear half the herb butter on to the fish, making sure that it goes into the cuts. Pre-heat the grill, and grill the fish for 4 minutes, then turn the fish over, spread the other sides with the butter as before, and grill the other side for 4 minutes. Serve immediately, with the juices from the grill pan poured over the fish.

RECIPE

WELSH SALMON STEAKS WITH GREEN BUTTER

This recipe for fresh salmon steaks baked in the oven with herb-flavoured butter is enough for four people – increase the quantities for more.

> 4 salmon steaks
> 2 lemon slices, cut into halves
> Salt and freshly ground black pepper, to taste
>
> For the green butter:
> 75g/3oz butter, softened to room temperature
> 1 fresh spinach leaf
> 3 sprigs of fresh parsley
> 2 sprigs of fresh mint
> A pinch of salt

Chop the spinach, parsley and mint very finely, then mix into the softened butter with a wooden spoon, beating it well so that everything is well combined. Season to taste with a pinch of salt. Spoon the green butter mixture on to a piece of greaseproof paper and roll it up to form a sausage shape. Twist the ends together, wrap in cling film and place in the freezer or ice box of the fridge for 20 minutes, until it is firm.

Pre-heat the oven to 190°C/375°F/Gas Mark 5. Cut out four pieces of foil each big enough to encase a salmon steak, grease them lightly and place a salmon steak in the centre of each piece of foil. Lightly season the salmon steaks with salt and freshly ground black pepper. Remove the green butter from the freezer, unwrap it and slice it into 8 rounds. Place two rounds of the green butter on top of each salmon steak with one of the lemon pieces between them. Bring up the edges of the foil to encase each piece of salmon in a foil parcel and crinkle the edges to seal firmly. Place the salmon parcels on a baking sheet and cook in the pre-heated oven for 20-25 minutes.

Remove from the oven, undo the foil and slide the salmon steaks with their topping on to warmed serving plates, pour the juices from the parcel on to each salmon steak and serve.

TAN-Y-LLYN, THE LAKE 1895 36481

RECIPE

TROUT WRAPPED IN BACON –
BRITHYLL MEWN CIG MOCH

This way of cooking trout has been traditional in Wales for hundreds of years. The bacon bastes the fish during cooking, keeping it moist and adding flavour.

  4 medium trout, cleaned and gutted
  50g/2oz butter
  4 sprigs of tarragon, finely chopped
  2 sprigs of marjoram, finely chopped
  4 tablespoonfuls finely chopped onions or chives
  1 teaspoonful freshly ground black pepper
  8 long rashers of smoked streaky bacon
  2 tablespoonfuls finely chopped fresh parsley, to garnish

Mix together all the chopped herbs except the parsley, and add plenty of freshly ground black pepper. Put a quarter of the butter into the cavity of each fish, and press into it a quarter of the chopped herbs mixture. Cut the rind off the bacon rashers. Stretch each bacon slice using the back of a knife, then wind two slices spirally around each fish, beginning where the head joins the body and ending at the tail end. Lay the bacon-wrapped fish in a grill pan, with all the heads facing the same way, and cook under a pre-heated, very hot grill for 3-4 minutes, then turn and cook the other side for a further 3-4 minutes. If the bacon begins to burn, lower the grill pan a little, but not the heat. Test with a metal skewer to check when the trout are cooked through, then serve sprinkled with chopped fresh parsley.

Alternatively, the trout can be oven-baked if preferred. Place the fish in a lightly greased, shallow baking dish with the loose ends of the bacon tucked underneath to prevent them unwinding. Bake in a pre-heated oven (200°C/400°F/Gas Mark 6) for 15-20 minutes, until the trout flesh flakes easily when tested with the point of a hot knife and the bacon is crisp and beginning to brown. Sprinkle with chopped fresh parsley before serving.

RECIPE

SEA TROUT, OR SEWIN (SIWIN), WITH HERBED MAYONNAISE SAUCE

Sea trout from the fast-flowing rivers of Wales are called sewin in Wales ('siwin' in Welsh), and are delicious, with pink flesh and a delicate flavour. This recipe for a whole sewin with a green herb sauce serves four.

> One cleaned sea trout (sewin), weighing about 900g/2 lbs
> 3 tablespoonfuls lemon juice
> 50g/2oz butter
> 1 bunch of watercress, washed and with the stalks cut off, finely chopped
> 115g/4oz fresh spinach leaves, roughly chopped
> 3 tablespoonfuls fresh parsley, finely chopped
> 2 tablespoonfuls fresh chervil, finely chopped
> 1 teaspoonful fresh dill, finely chopped
> 150ml/ ¼ pint mayonnaise
> Fresh herbs to garnish

Pre-heat the oven to 180ºC/350ºF/Gas Mark 4. Place the fish in the centre of a large piece of greased foil. Add 2 tablespoonfuls of the lemon juice, then dot the fish with 25g/1oz of the butter, cut into small pieces. Seal the foil, weigh the fish and place it on a baking sheet. Calculate the cooking time at 10 minutes per 450g (1 lb), and bake the fish in the pre-heated oven for the appropriate time, until tender. Remove the fish from the foil, reserving the cooking liquor, and carefully remove the skin from the fish whilst it is still warm. Arrange the fish on a serving dish, then leave to cool.

To make the sauce, put the reserved cooking liquor and the remaining butter in a saucepan and heat gently until the butter has melted. Add the chopped watercress, spinach, parsley, chervil and dill, then cook gently for 2-3 minutes, until softened. Liquidize the sauce in a food processor or blender until it is smooth. Transfer the sauce to a bowl, add the remaining lemon juice and leave it to cool. Fold in the mayonnaise using a large metal spoon, then turn the sauce into a small serving bowl and chill until required. When the fish is cold, garnish it with fresh herbs, and serve with the herb sauce.

RECIPE

WELSH HERRING SUPPER – SWPER SCADAN

In the days when herring were plentiful, these fish were landed in great quantities in Wales, particularly at Aberystwyth after the harbour was developed in the 18th century. The fishermen of the town brought in large numbers of herring for salting between September and November. The fish were then packed in barrels and transported by land for sale beyond the borders of Wales.

> 6-8 herrings, cleaned, scaled and filleted
> 1 tablespoonful made mustard
> Salt and freshly ground black pepper
> 25g/1oz butter, cut into small pieces
> 900g/2 lbs potatoes, peeled and thinly sliced
> 1 large onion, sliced
> 2 cooking apples, peeled, cored and diced
> 1 dessertspoonful of fresh sage, finely chopped

Pre-heat the oven to 180ºC/350ºF/Gas Mark 4.

Spread the inside of each herring fillet with mustard, season with salt and freshly ground black pepper, and roll it up.

Grease an ovenproof dish and place half the potato slices in a layer in the dish. Cover with a layer of onions, and then a layer of apples. Lay the rolled herrings on top, season with more salt and pepper and sprinkle with the sage. Cover with a further layer of the remaining potatoes. Pour on enough boiling water to come halfway up the dish.

Dot with butter, cover with foil and bake in the pre-heated oven for 45 minutes. Remove the foil and cook for a further 30 minutes, to brown the potatoes.

RECIPE

MACKEREL WITH WALNUT STUFFING

For many centuries great shoals of both herring and mackerel were caught off the Welsh coast, and the Cardigan Bay Seafood Festival is held around the harbour at Aberaeron in Dyfed in July each year, with stalls all along the harbourside selling a variety of seafood, much of it locally caught. Aberaeron also hosts an annual Mackerel Festival in late August/early September, to celebrate the importance of this fish to the economy of the town. It is said that in the 1880s the fishermen of Aberaeron and New Quay once caught over 1,000,000 mackerel over 2 nights. The fish were sold for a farthing each, and what remained unsold from the mammoth catch was used on the fields as fertiliser. This recipe can also be made with herring, if preferred.

> 4 mackerel, cleaned and boned, with their heads and tails removed
> 75g/3oz butter
> 1 medium onion, finely chopped
> 50g/2oz fresh breadcrumbs
> 50g/2oz shelled walnut pieces, roughly chopped
> 1 tablespoonful made mustard
> Salt and freshly ground black pepper
> The grated zest and juice of 1 lemon
> 3 tablespoonfuls fresh mixed herbs such as chives, parsley, sage, thyme, finely chopped
> Lemon wedges, to garnish

Melt 15g (½ oz) of the butter in a saucepan, add the finely chopped onion and fry for about 5 minutes, stirring occasionally, until the onion is softened and transparent. Mix together the breadcrumbs, chopped walnuts, mustard, lemon zest, 1 tablespoonful of lemon juice and the mixed herbs. Add the onion and season to taste, then mix it all together, to make the stuffing. Open the mackerel fillets and lay them skin side down. Press the stuffing mixture evenly over each fillet. Fold the mackerel fillets back in half and slash the skin several times. Melt the remaining butter in a large frying pan, add the fish and fry for about 10 minutes, turning them once, until they are tender and browned on each side. Serve with lemon wedges.

Alternatively, the mackerel can be oven-cooked, if preferred: arrange the mackerel in a lightly greased shallow baking tin and bake in a pre-heated oven at 190°C/375°/Gas Mark 5 for 20-25 minutes.

TENBY, LLANGWM FISHWIVES 1890 28093

RECIPE

COCKLE PIE – PASTAI COCOS

For centuries, cockles have been gathered around the shores of the Gower peninsula. Traditionally they were mainly collected by tough and redoubtable cockle-women, famous for their resilience in being able to work in all weather conditions, bent double for hours on end as they searched the cold sands for the tell-tale pair of small holes which betray the cockle's presence just below the surface.

> 900ml/1½ pints (volume measure) cooked fresh cockles
> 600ml/1 pint milk
> 225g/8oz streaky bacon rashers
> 115g/4oz fresh breadcrumbs
> 75g/3oz Caerphilly cheese, grated
> 50g/2oz plain flour
> 25g/1oz butter
> 1 onion, peeled and finely chopped
> 4 tablespoonfuls dry white wine
> 3 tablespoonfuls finely chopped fresh chives

Remove the rind from the bacon rashers and chop them into small pieces. Melt the butter in a large saucepan, add the chopped bacon and onion and cook gently for about 5 minutes, until the onion is softened and transparent. Stir in the flour and cook gently for a further minute, stirring constantly, then remove the pan from the heat. Gradually add the milk, a little at a time, stirring well with each addition so that no lumps are formed. Return the pan to the heat and bring to the boil, stirring continuously, until the sauce has thickened and is smooth. Stir in the cockles, wine and chopped chives, and simmer for a few minutes.

Pre-heat the grill. Mix the breadcrumbs and grated cheese together. Pour the cockle mixture into a warmed ovenproof dish, then sprinkle the cheese and breadcrumb mixture over the top. Place the dish under the hot grill for about 5 minutes, until the topping is crisp and golden brown. Serve immediately.

RECIPE

MUSSELS WITH CIDER AND LEEKS

Conwy in Gwynedd, on the banks of the Menai Strait between north Wales and the island of Anglesey, is famous for its mussels, harvested from the mussel beds in the estuary of the River Conwy and still gathered in the traditional way. The freshwater mussels found upstream of the river have also given Conwy another claim to fame, as a source of pearls – Conwy was once one of the most important pearl fisheries in the country, and in the early 19th century over 4 kilos of pearls were sent from here each week to London jewellers. A traditional way of eating mussels from the Menai Strait area of north Wales is to serve them taken out of their shells, in a sauce made from milk and the cooking liquor which has been thickened with balls made from oatmeal flour. This alternative Welsh recipe serves them in their shells, cooked in a cider and leek sauce. These amounts will serve 4 people.

2kg/4½ lbs mussels in their shells
1 medium sized leek, trimmed, washed and diced into
   very small pieces
2 shallots or small onions, very finely chopped
4 cloves of garlic, crushed or very finely chopped
2 tablespoons of finely chopped fresh parsley
50g/2oz butter
300ml/ ½ pint good quality dry cider
Salt and freshly ground black pepper to taste

Scrub the mussels well in cold water from a running tap, and discard any that have cracked or broken shells and also any with open shells that do not close when given a sharp tap. Use a sharp knife to remove the 'beards' (black tufts) attached to the shells.

LLANDUDNO, ON THE BEACH 1890 23242

Melt the butter in a very large pan and add the finely chopped leek, shallots or onions and garlic, and cook, stirring occasionally, over a medium heat until soft and tender. Add the cider, and bring to the boil. Add the prepared mussels and half the chopped parsley, then cover the pan with its lid and continue to cook over a high heat for 5-8 minutes until the mussels have opened, shaking the pan occasionally. At the end of the cooking time strain the mussels over a bowl, reserving the cooking liquor, and discard any mussels that have not opened – these are not safe to eat, so do not attempt to prise them open.

Divide the opened mussels into deep wide bowls, or one large serving dish. Season the reserved cooking liquor with salt and pepper to taste, and pour it over the cooked mussels. Serve the mussels immediately, garnished with the remaining chopped parsley and with plenty of crusty bread to mop up the liquid.

RECIPE

HONEYED WELSH LAMB – CIG OEN CYMREIG Â MÊL

Full-flavoured Welsh lamb is amongst the best and least adulterated meat that can be bought in Britain, and is one of the most famous specialities of Wales. This recipe gives a spicy gloss to a joint of roast lamb, and the residue in the roasting tin makes a delicious gravy. Use Welsh-produced honey and cider if you can, for a true flavour of Wales!

> 1.5-2kg/3-4 lbs joint of Welsh spring lamb, leg or shoulder
> Salt and pepper
> 1 teaspoonful ground ginger
> 1 dessertspoonful dried rosemary
> 2 good tablespoonfuls runny honey
> 300ml/ ½ pint dry cider

Pre-heat the oven to 200ºC/400ºF/Gas Mark 6. Rub all over the lamb with the salt, pepper and ginger, then place the joint in a roasting tin or dish and sprinkle the rosemary all over it. Dribble the honey all over the lamb, and pour the cider around it.

Calculate the cooking time of the lamb, allowing 25 minutes per ½ kg (1 lb) weight of the joint, plus 20 minutes extra. Cook the lamb near the top of the pre-heated oven for 30 minutes, then baste the meat and reduce the oven temperature to 180ºC/350ºF/Gas Mark 4 for the remaining cooking time. Baste the meat every 20 minutes or so, adding a little extra cider if necessary.

When the lamb is cooked, transfer it to a warmed dish and keep hot whilst you make a gravy to accompany it, using the residue in the roasting tin. Serve with new potatoes and seasonal vegetables.

CADAIR IDRIS, FROM CROSS FOXES c1960 C1373

RECIPE

LOIN OF PORK WITH CABBAGE CAKE

In the past the pig formed a mainstay of the diet for most Welsh people. This recipe comes from the Welsh Marches, but in both rural areas and the mining valleys of Wales there would be a 'twlc' or pig-sty at the bottom of many gardens. Ask your butcher to chine the pork, remove the skin and score the joint for you.

> A loin of pork, about 1.5kg/3½ lbs in weight, chined and scored
> 4 tablespoonfuls plain flour
> Salt to taste
> 1 tablespoonful dripping, lard or cooking fat
> 300ml/ ½ pint stock
> 1 white cabbage, about 1kg (2lbs 4oz) in weight, very finely shredded
> 25g/1oz butter
> 1 onion, very finely chopped
> 50g/2oz sultanas
> Salt and freshly ground black pepper
> 4 eating apples, peeled, cored and cut into quarters
> 1 tablespoonful finely chopped fresh parsley

Pre-heat the oven to 200ºC/400ºF/Gas Mark 6. Rub the pork with flour and salt and place in a hot roasting tin in the oven, with a tablespoonful of dripping, lard or cooking fat. Cook the pork for 1½ hours, basting very soon after it has put in the oven, and twice more during cooking.

About half an hour after the pork has been put in the oven, blanch the shredded cabbage in boiling water for 2 minutes, then drain it and set aside. Melt the butter in a shallow, flameproof casserole dish and cook the onion gently until it is soft and transparent. Remove the cooked onion, mix it with the cabbage and stir in the sultanas. Season to taste with salt and freshly ground black pepper. Put the apple quarters into the bottom of the casserole dish in which the onion was cooked; put the cabbage and onion mixture on top and press it down firmly. Cover the dish closely with foil and then with its lid, and cook very gently on top of the cooker for 15 minutes. Transfer the cabbage cake to the oven, with the pork, for the last 40 minutes of the meat's cooking time.

When the pork has cooked, place it on a warmed dish and keep hot whilst you make the gravy. Discard most of the fat from the roasting tin, then stir 1 tablespoonful of flour into the remainder. Place the tin over heat and gradually add the stock, a little at a time, stirring continually so that no lumps are formed. Bring to the boil and boil for 2 minutes, stirring constantly, until the gravy has thickened. Season to taste, and serve in a jug or gravy boat with the pork and the cabbage cake. Turn out the cabbage cake onto a hot dish by running a knife round the sides of the casserole and then turning it upside down on to the inverted dish. Sprinkle with the chopped parsley, and serve with the pork and gravy.

PONTYPRIDD, MARKET STREET 1899
43605

CARMARTHEN, THE GUILDHALL 1906 53738

RECIPE

THE MISER'S FEAST – FFEST Y CYBYDD

This tasty dish is said to have been popular in Carmarthenshire in the past. The miser of the title was supposed to eat the potatoes and onion on the first day the dish was cooked, mashed up in the liquid, and keep the meat to eat the next day with boiled potatoes. Long, slow cooking is the secret to making this flavoursome dish.

> 450g/1 lb belly pork rashers or thin pork chops
> 2-3 large or 4-6 small potatoes
> 2 large onions
> 600ml/1 pint chicken or vegetable stock
> Salt and freshly ground black pepper

Pre-heat the oven to 180°C/350°F/Gas Mark 4. Peel and thinly slice the potatoes and onions. Starting with the potatoes, place alternate layers of sliced potatoes and onions into a greased ovenproof dish or casserole, ending with a final layer of potatoes, seasoning each layer lightly as you go. Pour over the stock. Place the belly pork slices or chops on the top. Cover the dish with its lid and bake in the pre-heated oven for 2½ hours, then turn the meat over, remove the cover and cook, uncovered, for a further 30 minutes to allow the meat to brown.

RECIPE

WELSH ROAST POTATOES AND BACON
– TATWS RHOST

This simple supper dish is still a favourite in Wales. In past years it would have been cooked in a 'ffwrn fach', a little pot oven which stood over an open fire.

> 900g/2 lb potatoes, peeled and sliced
> 1 bunch spring onions, trimmed and sliced
> 6 thick rashers of bacon
> 80ml/3 fl oz water
> Salt and freshly ground black pepper

Pre-heat the oven to 190°C/375°F/Gas Mark 5.

Place the sliced potatoes in a layer in a greased, shallow ovenproof dish, and cover them with the sliced spring onions. Lay the bacon rashers over the potatoes, and season to taste with salt and freshly ground black pepper.

Pour in the water, cover the dish with foil and cook in the pre-heated oven for 45 minutes, then remove the foil and bake, uncovered, for a further 15 minutes.

SWANSEA, HIGH STREET 1893 32720

RECIPE

WELSH RABBIT (OR RAREBIT) – CAWS POBI

Cheese-making has a long tradition in Wales. Milk from goats and sheep as well as cows was used in the past to make a variety of cheeses, and it seems that some of these early cheeses were immersed in brine for part of their production process. Cheeses were considered so valuable in 10th-century Wales that they were included in divorce settlements when Hywel Dda ('Hywel the Good') codified Welsh law. Any cheese that was still in brine in the family home at the time the couple separated was considered to be the property of the wife, whilst any cheese which was hung up in the home, and had therefore finished its production process, went to the husband. This well-known supper dish is made from toast and a flavoured cheese sauce. Adding ale or beer improves the flavour, but milk can be used if preferred. Despite its name, Welsh Rabbit does not contain any meat, and is also known as 'Welsh Rarebit' – although 'Rabbit' seems to have been the original name. It can also be served with a fried or poached egg on top, when it is known as Buck Rabbit. The success of this dish lies in cooking it over a low heat until the cheese has melted.

> 4 thick slices of bread
> 50g/2oz butter
> 225g/8oz mature hard cheese of choice, grated
> 1 teaspoonful mustard powder
> A few drops of Worcestershire Sauce
> 2-3 tablespoonfuls brown ale, beer or milk, as preferred
> Salt and pepper

Pre-heat the grill. Toast the bread slices on both sides, then keep them warm until needed. Melt the butter in a heavy-bottomed saucepan. Add the grated cheese, mustard powder and salt and pepper to taste, and stir over a gentle heat until the cheese melts. Gradually add the ale, beer or milk, stirring all the time until the mixture is very well blended. Spread the toast slices with the mixture and place under the pre-heated hot grill until the topping is bubbling and golden.

RECIPE

GLAMORGAN SAUSAGES – SELSIG MORGANNWG

The town of Caerphilly near Cardiff has given its name to a hard, crumbly white cheese but it was not actually made there – Caerphilly cheese was so-named because it was sold in the town's market, and it became popular with the growing population of the industrialising valleys. Nowadays this cheese is made only in England's West Country and no longer in Wales, but Caerphilly nevertheless holds a famous Big Cheese Festival each year, and Caerphilly cheese is still the preferred choice for making these meatless sausages.

150g/5oz fresh breadcrumbs
150g/5oz grated Caerphilly cheese
1 small leek, very finely chopped
1 tablespoonful chopped fresh parsley
Leaves from 1 sprig of thyme, chopped
2 eggs
1½ teaspoonfuls mustard powder
3 tablespoonfuls milk
Plain flour, for coating
1 tablespoonful oil
1 tablespoonful melted butter
Salt and pepper

Mix the breadcrumbs, cheese, leek, herbs and seasoning. Whisk the eggs with the mustard and reserve 2 tablespoonfuls of the mixture. Stir the rest into the cheese mixture with enough milk to bind. Divide the cheese mixture into eight and form into sausage shapes.

Dip the sausages in the reserved beaten egg to coat them on all sides. Season the flour, then roll the sausages in it to give them a light, even coating. Chill the sausages for about 30 minutes until they are firm.

Pre-heat the grill and oil the grill rack. Mix the oil and melted butter together and brush this over the sausages. Grill the sausages for about 5-10 minutes, turning them carefully, until they are golden brown all over. These can be served hot or cold.

CARDIFF, TRAFFIC IN QUEEN STREET 1893 32678x

GLOVE & SHEARS HOTEL
E.T.REES.
WINE & SPIRIT VAULTS

RECIPE

WELSH ONION CAKE – TEISEN NIONOD

7 medium sized potatoes, peeled and thinly sliced
3 onions, peeled and thinly sliced
115g/4oz butter or margarine, cut into small pieces
Salt and freshly ground black pepper
115g/4oz hard cheese of choice, grated

Pre-heat the oven to 150°C/300°F/Gas Mark 5.

Dry the potato slices on kitchen paper to remove excess moisture. Grease a loaf tin or a cake tin and place the sliced potatoes and onions in layers in the tin, beginning and ending with a layer of potatoes. Dot each layer with a few pieces of butter, and also the top layer of potatoes, and season each layer to taste as you go with a little salt and pepper.

Cover the tin with aluminium foil and bake in the pre-heated oven for 1½ hours, removing the foil cover for the last half-hour for the cake to brown.

When cooked, turn the cake onto an ovenproof serving dish, sprinkle the top with the grated cheese and place under a pre-heated hot grill for a couple of minutes, until the cheese is melted and bubbling, before serving.

ABERGAVENNY, CROSS STREET 1898 41675

ANGLESEY EGGS – ŴYAU YNYS MÔN

Anglesey ('Ynys Môn' in Welsh) is a large island extending into the Irish Sea which is separated from north Wales by the Menai Strait. At the time of the Roman conquest of Britain in the first century AD the island was a centre of the Druidic priesthood, and was attacked by the Romans in AD61. The Roman writer Tacitus described the scene as the legionaries prepared to attack: 'On the coastline, a line of warriors of the opposition was stationed, mainly made up of armed men, amongst them women, with their hair blowing in the wind, while they were carrying torches. Druids were amongst them, shouting terrifying spells, their hands raised towards the heavens…'. But the spells were in vain – the Romans were victorious, massacred the Druids and burnt their sacred oak groves. The Menai Strait is now spanned by Thomas Telford's famous suspension bridge, and thousands of more peaceable visitors cross the water to the island each year for holidays. This recipe from Anglesey makes a tasty tea or supper dish.

BEAUMARIS, CHURCH STREET 1911 63301x

RECIPE

450g/1 lb hot mashed potatoes
300ml/ ½ pint milk
115g/4oz hard cheese of choice, grated
75g/3oz butter
8 eggs, hard-boiled and peeled
6 small leeks, washed, trimmed and sliced into small
   pieces
1 tablespoonful plain flour
Half a teaspoonful made mustard
A pinch of grated nutmeg
Salt and freshly ground black pepper

Pre-heat the oven to 200°C/400°F/Gas Mark 6. Boil the sliced leeks in water for 8-10 minutes, then drain well. Combine the leeks with the mashed potato and half the butter, season to taste with salt and pepper, and mix well until the mixture is fluffy. Turn the mixture into a greased ovenproof baking dish. Melt 25g (1oz) of the remaining butter in a saucepan. Stir in the flour, and cook gently over a low heat for 2 minutes, stirring continuously. Gradually stir in the milk, a little at a time so that no lumps are formed, then increase the heat, add the grated nutmeg and most of the grated cheese and bring to the boil, stirring constantly, until the sauce has thickened. Reduce the heat, season to taste, then simmer gently for 2 minutes, stirring. Cut the hard-boiled eggs in half and arrange them on top of the leek and potato mixture. Cover with the cheese sauce, sprinkle the remaining grated cheese on top and dot with small pieces of the remaining butter. Bake in the pre-heated oven for 20-25 minutes, or until the topping is golden brown.

RECIPE

LAVERBREAD BREAKFAST – BARA LAWR BRECWAST

The edible Laver seaweed (porphyra umbilicalis) is collected around the coast of Wales (especially the Gower peninsula and the Pembrokeshire coastline) and is very nutritious, being rich in vitamins and minerals. After being gathered from the rocks at low tide, it needs to be rinsed in several changes of fresh water to get rid of any sand and grit. When freshly picked it is almost purple in colour, but after it has been cooked (by boiling for about 20 minutes) it becomes a dark bright green. The resulting spinach-like mass is the true laverbread, which can be used for sauces (laverbead and orange sauce is excellent with salmon or duck) or for making laverbread cakes, a favourite Welsh breakfast dish served with bacon. Fresh laverbead is sold from vans and stalls around Welsh towns and villages, and nowadays canned or dried laverbread can also be bought in many supermarkets or health food shops.

> 450g/1 lb laverbread
> 115g/4oz fine oatmeal
> 6 rashers of smoked back bacon
> Lard or bacon fat for frying

Mix the laverbread and the oatmeal together. Form the mixture into small cakes, about 5cm (2 inches) across and 2cm (¾ inch) thick, then flatten and shape them with a palette knife.

Fry the bacon rashers in a little lard or fat, then remove them from the pan and keep them warm. Drop the laverbread cakes into the hot fat left in the frying pan, and fry them fairly fast for 2 minutes on each side, shaping and patting them as they fry. Lift the cakes out of the pan very carefully, using a wide palette knife or slice, and serve with the bacon rashers.

BARRY ISLAND, WHITMORE BAY 1910 62559

RECIPE

LEEK FLAN – TARTEN GENNIN

There are several theories about how the leek became a Welsh emblem, but they are all linked with battles fought between Welsh forces and Saxon (or English) foes. Legend says that that the Welsh leader (some tales say it was St David, others that it was King Cadwallawn) ordered his soldiers to gather the wild leeks growing on the battlefield and wear them on their caps or helmets, so they could identify themselves in the confusion of the fray. The Welsh were victorious, and thereafter adopted the leek as their national emblem in commemoration of the battle. There is a Welsh saying, 'Wear a leek in your cap, but also be sure to have one in your heart'.

> 175g/6oz shortcrust pastry
> 6 large leeks, trimmed and thoroughly washed
> 25g/1oz butter
> 150g/5oz bacon rashers with their rinds removed,
>   chopped into small pieces
> 4 eggs, beaten
> 300ml/ ½ pint milk or cream
> Salt and freshly ground black pepper
> 75g/3oz hard cheese of choice, grated

Pre-heat the oven to 200ºC/400ºF/Gas Mark 6, and place a baking tray in the oven to heat up. Roll out the pastry on a lightly floured surface, and use it to line a greased, shallow 23cm (9 inch) flan dish or tin. Prick the pastry all over with a fork to allow steam to escape during cooking. Place a piece of greaseproof paper with some baking beans on the pastry base, place the dish or tin on the pre-heated baking tray in the oven and bake blind for 15 minutes (this helps the pastry base to cook through). Remove from the oven, and take out the greaseproof paper and baking beans. Reduce the oven temperature to 180°C/350°F/Gas Mark 4.

Chop the washed and trimmed leeks into 2.5cm (1 inch) pieces. Heat the butter in a saucepan and cook the leeks over a very low heat with lid on the pan until they are soft. Spread the leeks in the pre-baked pastry case, and arrange the bacon pieces on top. Beat the eggs with the milk or cream, and season to taste with freshly ground black pepper and a little salt. Pour the mixture into the pastry case and sprinkle the grated cheese over the top. Put the flan into the middle or lower part of the pre-heated oven and bake for 30-35 minutes. Serve hot or cold.

WELSH DAFFODIL

The national flower of Wales is the daffodil. The daffodil is thought to have been chosen as a Welsh emblem because of the similarity of its name to Dafydd, the Welsh name for David, the patron saint of Wales. St David (or Dewi in Welsh) was a 6th-century monk who founded the abbey at St Davids in Pembrokeshire. An extremely popular saint, his shrine was a major centre for pilgrimages in the Middle Ages. St David's Day (March 1st) is the Welsh national day, when it is traditional to wear a leek or daffodil in your buttonhole. A Welsh tradition says that the person who sees the first flowering daffodil of the spring will be lucky enough to receive more gold than silver during the coming year.

HAVERFORDWEST, FETCHING THE WATER 1890 27951x

RECIPE

PUNCHNEP

This Welsh dish combines potatoes and turnips to make a buttery purée that is then dotted with pools of hot cream. To obtain the authentic flavour of punchnep, it is essential to boil the potatoes and turnips in separate saucepans, and then to also drain and mash them separately.

> 450g/1 lb potatoes, peeled and chopped into large pieces
> 450g/1 lb young turnips, peeled and chopped into large pieces
> 50g/2oz butter
> Salt and freshly ground black pepper
> 4 tablespoonfuls cream

Put the potato and turnip pieces into separate saucepans, and cover with water. Bring to the boil, then reduce the heat and cook until the vegetables are soft and tender. Drain well, then mash the potatoes and turnips separately, with half the butter added to each.

Combine the two mashed vegetables well together, beating the mixture thoroughly until a light, soft purée is formed. Season the punchnep to taste, with salt and freshly ground black pepper.

Pile the punchnep into a heated serving dish. Make 6-8 'wells' in the mixture with the handle of a wooden spoon, and fill each 'well' with cream. Serve the punchnep immediately, whilst it is hot.

HARLECH, THE CASTLE AND GOLF LINKS 1908 60251

RECIPE

TOFFEE TART – TEISEN TAFFI

This is a dessert for those with a very sweet tooth! The dates melt down in the syrup as the tart cooks, producing a delicious sticky toffee filling in a sweet pastry case. It is best eaten warm, a few minutes after cooking.

<u>For the pastry:</u>
175g/6oz plain flour
50g/2oz butter or margarine
25g/1oz lard
50g/2oz caster sugar
A pinch of salt
2-3 tablespoonfuls cold milk

<u>For the filling:</u>
175g/6oz dried stoned dates, minced or chopped into very small pieces
3-4 tablespoonfuls of golden syrup
25g/1oz rolled oats
25g/1oz butter or margarine, cut into small pieces

Sift the flour and salt into a bowl, stir in the sugar and add the butter or margarine and lard, cut into small pieces. With your fingertips, rub the fats into the flour until the mixture resembles fine breadcrumbs. Stir in 2-3 tablespoonfuls of cold milk, enough to allow the mixture to be gathered together into a smooth ball of dough. Knead lightly until the dough is smooth and elastic, and leave in a cool place to 'rest' for about 15 minutes.

Pre-heat the oven to 190°C/375°F/Gas Mark 5. Grease a 20-22cm (8-9 inch) flan tin or pie plate. Roll out the pastry on a lightly floured surface and use it to line the prepared flan tin or plate, and flute or crimp the edge. Spread the bottom of the tart with the minced or chopped dates. Gently warm the golden syrup in a saucepan, then pour it evenly over the dates. Sprinkle with the rolled oats, and dot the surface with small knobs of butter.

Bake in the pre-heated oven for 25-30 minutes, until the pastry is golden brown and cooked through. Remove from the oven and leave to cool and set for five minutes before serving warm with custard or cream – do not serve piping hot from the oven.

RECIPE

WELSH BREAD PUDDING – PWDIN BARA

Welsh bread pudding is packed with fruit and spices, and is an excellent way of using up stale bread. It can be served warm as a pudding, with custard or cream, or cold, cut into squares, at teatime.

> 225g/8oz stale bread
> 300ml/ ½ pint milk
> 50g/2oz candied peel
> Grated peel of one orange
> Grated peel of one lemon
> 115g/4oz currants
> 50g/2oz sultanas
> 75g/3oz shredded suet
> 50g/2oz demerara sugar
> 2 level teaspoonfuls ground mixed spice
> 1 large egg
> A little milk, if necessary
> Butter or margarine, for greasing
> Freshly grated nutmeg to finish
> Caster sugar to finish

Cut away all the crust from the bread. Break the bread into small pieces, place it in a large mixing bowl, pour over the milk and leave it all to soak for 30 minutes (overnight is even better). Finely chop the candied peel and add to the bread with the grated orange and lemon peel, and mix well. Add the dried fruit, suet, demerara sugar and mixed spice and combine well. Beat the egg and stir it into the mixture, which should have a dropping consistency – if necessary, add a dessertspoonful or so of milk to soften it.

Pre-heat the oven to 180°C/350°F/Gas Mark 4.

Spoon the mixture into a well-greased 1.2 litre (2 pint) pie dish and grate a little fresh nutmeg over it. Bake on the middle shelf of the pre-heated oven for 1¾ - 2 hours, or until the top is nicely browned. Remove from the oven and dredge with caster sugar.

RECIPE

MONMOUTH PUDDING – PWDIN MYNWY

Use whatever fruit is available for this pudding, but apples or plums are particularly nice. Alternatively, jam can be used instead of the cooked fruit.

> 75g/3oz sugar
> 25g/1oz butter or margarine
> Grated zest of 1 lemon
> 450m/ ¾ pint milk
> 175g/6oz fresh breadcrumbs
> 3 eggs, separated
> 175g/6oz cooked fruit, such as apples, plums, peaches,
> rhubarb, pears (or any jam of choice, if preferred)

Pre-heat the oven to 170°C/325°F/Gas Mark 3.

Grease a shallow ovenproof pudding dish, or 4 individual ovenproof dishes if preferred. Place the butter or margarine, lemon zest, 25g (1oz) of the sugar and the milk in a saucepan and slowly heat to boiling point, stirring. Place the breadcrumbs in a mixing bowl and pour on the hot milk mixture. Leave to stand for 15 minutes. Stir the beaten egg yolks into the breadcrumb mixture, then pour the mixture into the prepared dish or dishes (if you are using jam instead of fruit, pour in half the mixture, spread with half the jam, and then add the remaining mixture). Bake in the pre-heated oven for 30-40 minutes, until set, then remove from the oven and place a layer of cooked fruit (or the remaining jam) over the top.

Whisk the egg whites in a large mixing bowl until they are stiff and stand in peaks, then use a large metal spoon to fold in the remaining sugar. Cover the top of the pudding with this meringue mixture. Return the pudding to the oven and bake for a further 15-20 minutes, until the topping is lightly browned. Serve hot.

MONMOUTH, THE STREET 1891 28784

RECIPE

SNOWDON PUDDING – PWDIN ERYRI

Snowdon in Gwynedd is the highest mountain in Wales, rising to 1085 metres (3,565 feet). Its Welsh name is 'Yr Wyddfa', said to mean 'the barrow' (a burial mound) and legend says that a giant called Rhita Fawr who was slain by King Arthur lies buried beneath it. It was the Anglo-Saxons who gave the mountain the name of 'Snow-dun', meaning 'the hill of Snow'. Today the mountain gives its name to the Snowdonia National Park, a popular playground for outdoor sports enthusiasts.

> 225g/8oz shredded suet
> 25g/1oz cornflour
> 225g/8oz fresh breadcrumbs
> 175g/6oz lemon marmalade
> A pinch of salt
> A little butter, for greasing the pudding basin
> 6 eggs, beaten
> 175g/6oz soft brown sugar
> 115g/4oz raisins
> Grated zest of 2 lemons

Mix together all the dry ingredients in a large mixing bowl, reserving a handful of raisins. Add the eggs, and beat the mixture well until it is all well blended.

Grease a pudding basin with butter and spread the reserved raisins over the bottom. Pour the pudding mixture into the basin, and cover the basin with its lid or a large round of greased greaseproof paper or foil, pleated to allow room for the pudding to expand during cooking, tied down securely with string.

Place the pudding basin in a large saucepan and pour in enough boiling water to come halfway up the sides of the basin. Bring the water back to the boil, cover the pan with its lid and leave the pudding to steam for 2 hours – top up the pan with more boiling water when necessary during the cooking time, and take care not to let the pan boil dry. Serve the pudding hot, with custard or cream.

BEDDGELERT, SNOWDON 1931 84742A

NEWPORT, A TRAM IN COMMERCIAL STREET 1901 47896v

RECIPE

SPECKLED BREAD – BARA BRITH

The name of this rich, spicy tea bread describes its appearance, speckled with dried fruit that is made wonderfully juicy by soaking it in (milkless) tea before baking. This tea bread is very easy to make, but be warned – it is very more-ish!

> 1 mug of strong, hot, milkless tea
> 4 tablespoonfuls marmalade
> 175g/6oz mixed dried fruit – currants, sultanas, raisins
> 225g/8oz soft brown sugar
> 350g/12oz self-raising flour
> 2 large eggs, beaten
> Half a teaspoonful of mixed spice (more, if you like it)

Put the fruit and marmalade in a bowl and add the hot (milkless) tea. Cover the bowl and leave the fruit to soak in the tea for at least one hour, although overnight is best.

Pre-heat the oven to 160°C/325°F/Gas Mark 3. Grease a loaf tin, and line the bottom and the two short sides with a long strip of greaseproof or baking paper.

Add the sugar, flour, beaten eggs and mixed spice to the fruit mixture, combine everything together well, turn the mixture into a greased loaf tin and smooth the surface evenly. Bake in the pre-heated oven for about 1½ hours, until a skewer inserted into the loaf comes out clean. Leave the loaf in the tin for 15 minutes to settle, then turn out onto a wire rack and leave to cool completely.

This is delicious cut into slices and spread with butter.

RECIPE

WELSH CAKES – PICAU AR Y MAEN

These traditional delicacies are the famous bakestone (or griddle) cakes of south Wales. If you do not have a griddle, use a heavy frying pan. Welsh Cakes can be eaten either whole, just as they are and dusted with a little sugar, or with a dab of butter on top, or split and spread with jam.

225g/8oz self-raising flour
Half a teaspoonful ground cinnamon
A pinch of ground nutmeg
A pinch of salt
115g/4oz butter or margarine
75g/3oz caster sugar
75g/3oz mixed dried fruit – currants, raisins, sultanas
1 egg, beaten
A little milk
Sunflower oil or fat for frying

Sift the flour, cinnamon and nutmeg into a bowl, and add the salt. Cut the butter or margarine into small pieces and rub it into the flour until the mixture resembles fine breadcrumbs. Stir in the sugar and the dried fruit. Add the beaten egg and about 1 tablespoonful of milk, and mix it quickly to form a soft but firm dough – add a splash more milk if needed. Roll out the dough on a lightly-floured surface to about 5mm (¼ inch) thick. Use a biscuit cutter or an upturned glass to stamp out the dough into rounds.

Lightly grease a griddle or heavy frying pan with a little of the oil or fat. Heat to medium-hot, then add the cakes, in batches. Cook for about 2-3 minutes, until they are puffed up and golden brown and just firm, then turn the cakes and continue to cook until golden brown but still soft inside – about a further 2-3 minutes. Remove the cakes from the griddle or pan and sprinkle each cake with a little caster sugar. If you like, place a dot of butter on the top of each cake, and eat straight away, whilst they are still hot.

**TAN Y BWLCH, FFESTINIOG RAILWAY
THE STATION MISTRESS 1935** 86736

WREXHAM
HIGH STREET FROM THE WINSTAY ARMS
1895 36281

RECIPE

BRECON LIGHT CAKES

115g/4oz self-raising flour
2 eggs
50g/2oz caster sugar
2-3 tablespoonfuls of milk
2 tablespoonfuls orange juice
A good pinch of salt
25g/1oz butter or margarine, for frying
25g/1oz soft brown sugar to finish
A little extra orange juice, to finish

Beat the eggs with the orange juice. Sift the flour and salt into a mixing bowl, add the caster sugar and then the egg and orange juice mixture, and mix it all together well. Whisk in just enough milk to form a fairly thin batter mixture.

Heat a griddle or a large, heavy frying pan, and melt a little of the butter on it. Drop tablespoonfuls of the batter mixture onto the greased, hot griddle or pan, allowing enough room for them to spread to about 5-8cm (2-3 inches) across. Cook the cakes for a few minutes on each side, until they are golden brown on both sides. Remove from the pan, drain on kitchen paper and keep warm. Continue until all the mixture has been used, adding more butter or margarine to the griddle or pan when necessary. Serve the cakes whilst they are still warm, sprinkled with soft brown sugar and a few drops of orange juice.

RECIPE

ABERFFRAW CAKES – TEISENNAU ABERFFRO

The recipe for these small biscuit-like cakes comes from Aberffraw in the south of the island of Anglesey. Nowadays they are made as simple round biscuits marked with lines to imitate the markings of a scallop shell, but in past times the dough was actually moulded in a scallop shell, to make shell-shaped cakes. One of the explanations for this is a romantic legend that whilst a Welsh prince was holding his court in Aberffraw many centuries ago, his wife went for a walk along the beach, picked up a pretty scallop shell and asked for a cake to be baked for her in the same shape.

175g/6oz self-raising flour
115g/4oz butter
50g/2oz caster sugar
A little milk, if necessary
A little extra sugar, to finish

Pre-heat the oven to 190°C/375°F/Gas Mark 5. Melt the butter in a bowl over a saucepan of hot water and beat in the sugar. Gradually add the flour, mixing it well in – add a small amount of milk to the mixture if the dough is hard to work. Roll the dough out on a lightly floured surface to about 5mm (¼ inch) thickness. Stamp the dough into rounds using a biscuit cutter (this amount should make about 6-10 cakes, depending on the size of the cutter). Use a sharp non-serrated knife to lightly score decorative lines on the rounds in a fan shape, to imitate a scallop shell. Place the rounds on a greased baking sheet and bake in the pre-heated oven for about 15 minutes, or until they are golden brown. Turn out onto a wire rack to cool, and sprinkle with a little extra caster sugar. They can either be eaten as they are, or served spread with thick cream and jam.

FRANCIS FRITH

PIONEER VICTORIAN PHOTOGRAPHER

Francis Frith, founder of the world-famous photographic archive, was a complex and multi-talented man. A devout Quaker and a highly successful Victorian businessman, he was philosophical by nature and pioneering in outlook. By 1855 he had already established a wholesale grocery business in Liverpool, and sold it for the astonishing sum of £200,000, which is the equivalent today of over £15,000,000. Now in his thirties, and captivated by the new science of photography, Frith set out on a series of pioneering journeys up the Nile and to the Near East.

INTRIGUE AND EXPLORATION

He was the first photographer to venture beyond the sixth cataract of the Nile. Africa was still the mysterious 'Dark Continent', and Stanley and Livingstone's historic meeting was a decade into the future. The conditions for picture taking confound belief. He laboured for hours in his wicker dark-room in the sweltering heat of the desert, while the volatile chemicals fizzed dangerously in their trays. Back in London he exhibited his photographs and was 'rapturously cheered' by members of the Royal Society. His reputation as a photographer was made overnight.

VENTURE OF A LIFE-TIME

By the 1870s the railways had threaded their way across the country, and Bank Holidays and half-day Saturdays had been made obligatory by Act of Parliament. All of a sudden the working man and his family were able to enjoy days out, take holidays, and see a little more of the world.

With typical business acumen, Francis Frith foresaw that these new tourists would enjoy having souvenirs to commemorate their days out. For the next thirty years he travelled the country by train and by pony and trap, producing fine photographs of seaside resorts and beauty spots that were keenly bought by millions of Victorians. These prints were painstakingly pasted into family albums and pored over during the dark nights of winter, rekindling precious memories of summer excursions. Frith's studio was soon supplying retail shops all over the country, and by 1890 F Frith & Co had become the greatest specialist photographic publishing company in the world, with over 2,000 sales outlets, and pioneered the picture postcard.

FRANCIS FRITH'S LEGACY

Francis Frith had died in 1898 at his villa in Cannes, his great project still growing. By 1970 the archive he created contained over a third of a million pictures showing 7,000 British towns and villages.

Frith's legacy to us today is of immense significance and value, for the magnificent archive of evocative photographs he created provides a unique record of change in the cities, towns and villages throughout Britain over a century and more. Frith and his fellow studio photographers revisited locations many times down the years to update their views, compiling for us an enthralling and colourful pageant of British life and character.

We are fortunate that Frith was dedicated to recording the minutiae of everyday life. For it is this sheer wealth of visual data, the painstaking chronicle of changes in dress, transport, street layouts, buildings, housing and landscape that captivates us so much today, offering us a powerful link with the past and with the lives of our ancestors.

Computers have now made it possible for Frith's many thousands of images to be accessed almost instantly. The archive offers every one of us an opportunity to examine the places where we and our families have lived and worked down the years. Its images, depicting our shared past, are now bringing pleasure and enlightenment to millions around the world a century and more after his death.

For further information visit: www.francisfrith.com

INTERIOR DECORATION

Frith's photographs can be seen framed and as giant wall murals in thousands of pubs, restaurants, hotels, banks, retail stores and other public buildings throughout Britain. These provide interesting and attractive décor, generating strong local interest and acting as a powerful reminder of gentler days in our increasingly busy and frenetic world.

FRITH PRODUCTS

All Frith photographs are available as prints and posters in a variety of different sizes and styles. In the UK we also offer a range of other gift and stationery products illustrated with Frith photographs, although many of these are not available for delivery outside the UK – see our web site for more information on the products available for delivery in your country.

THE INTERNET

Over 100,000 photographs of Britain can be viewed and purchased on the Frith web site. The web site also includes memories and reminiscences contributed by our customers, who have personal knowledge of localities and of the people and properties depicted in Frith photographs. If you wish to learn more about a specific town or village you may find these reminiscences fascinating to browse. Why not add your own comments if you think they would be of interest to others? See **www.francisfrith.com**

PLEASE HELP US BRING FRITH'S PHOTOGRAPHS TO LIFE

Our authors do their best to recount the history of the places they write about. They give insights into how particular towns and villages developed, they describe the architecture of streets and buildings, and they discuss the lives of famous people who lived there. But however knowledgeable our authors are, the story they tell is necessarily incomplete.

Frith's photographs are so much more than plain historical documents. They are living proofs of the flow of human life down the generations. They show real people at real moments in history; and each of those people is the son or daughter of someone, the brother or sister, aunt or uncle, grandfather or grandmother of someone else. All of them lived, worked and played in the streets depicted in Frith's photographs.

We would be grateful if you would give us your insights into the places shown in our photographs: the streets and buildings, the shops, businesses and industries. Post your memories of life in those streets on the Frith website: what it was like growing up there, who ran the local shop and what shopping was like years ago; if your workplace is shown tell us about your working day and what the building is used for now. Read other visitors' memories and reconnect with your shared local history and heritage. With your help more and more Frith photographs can be brought to life, and vital memories preserved for posterity, and for the benefit of historians in the future.

Wherever possible, we will try to include some of your comments in future editions of our books. Moreover, if you spot errors in dates, titles or other facts, please let us know, because our archive records are not always completely accurate—they rely on 140 years of human endeavour and hand-compiled records. You can email us using the contact form on the website.

Thank you!

For further information, trade, or author enquiries
please contact us at the address below:

The Francis Frith Collection, Unit 6, Oakley Business Park, Wylye Road, Dinton, Wiltshire SP3 5EU.

Tel: +44 (0)1722 716 376 Fax: +44 (0)1722 716 881
e-mail: sales@francisfrith.co.uk **www.francisfrith.com**